MW00653366

Stop Selling

and

Start Marketing

STOP Selling

START Marketing

Stop Selling and Start Marketing

by

Tom Wright

Published by

Wright's Press

Published by Wright's Press
Porterville, California 93257

ISBN 0-9719535-0-3
Printed in the United States of America
Second Printing: March 2003
Third Printing: March 2006

Dedicated to my three girls
Judy, Jenny, Julie with all my love.

Special thanks to Helen Kennedy

START
Marketing

Preface

Selling is persuading someone to buy your product or service. Marketing is a planned approach whereby you locate people that have a propensity to need your product or service and help them fill their need. Marketing is a way to reach out to customers that want to be reached. A planned repeatable marketing program allows your organization to market on a perpetual basis. Marketing is an organized program, not a project you do once a month until you meet a quota.

STOP
Selling

START
Marketing

Chapter 1

Don't "sell", fulfill a need

The challenge is not selling something to someone, the challenge is to develop a way to have our clients want to come to us to fulfill or satisfy their needs. Over the years I've found that there are two types of sales that are made. One is through persuasion by the salesperson convincing the prospect that he or she needs the product or service. The other is not really a sale at all, but rather a fulfillment of the prospect's needs.

The salesperson can achieve similar results, however the ease in which the sale is made varies greatly. When someone needs a product or service, they are more than happy to help with the sale by giving feedback as to their needs and desires about the product or service they are interested in.

When the prospect is helping the salesperson tailor to their specific needs, the process can actually be very enjoyable. Conversely, if the salesperson is tying to persuade the customer to buy the product, the process becomes uneasy. In marketing, the key to consistent, predictable sales is to have a process that encourages the prospect to become involved in the sales process.

In all forms of selling, reaching the prospect through honest, heartfelt conversation will help the prospect understand the need for purchasing the product. Increased sales and stronger relationships will be a natural result of this process.

Developing relationships is the cornerstone to long term customers. These customers foster repeat sales and referrals. When a prospect realizes the need and appreciates being educated about your product, they are more than willing to have their friends and associates come to you for the same type of help.

Set yourself apart People do want to be informed and naturally want to share new information with their friends. This makes them feel like they are helping people, which helps them feel better in the process. Why not let them mention your name and help you grow your business. It's the little things you do that will help foster referrals and build a marketing network. Try to think of things that set you apart from the crowd. Whether it be an advertisement, taking donuts to a prospective customer, anything that sets you apart can help you be the one people think of when they need your service or product.

Don't over sell Over the years, I've been on the buying side of the fence on many purchases. Some have been positive but the majority were clumsy and unpolished presentations. On several occasions I've even felt sorry for the salesperson and tried to make it easier for them to present the product to me.

When my wife Judy and I first got married, we borrowed her mother's vacuum cleaner to vacuum our rented house. It was an old Kirby that must have weighed fifty pounds or more. But that vacuum actually lifted the carpet up off the floor. It was a quality vacuum. I'll never forget that. With all the different houses that we rented or owned, I've always thought that someday we would get a Kirby of our own .

About ten years ago, I contacted our local Kirby dealer and asked him to quote me a price on their latest model. The chain of events that followed was unbelievable. He insisted on coming out to my office to do a demonstration and explain the features of the G4 Kirby. I mentioned to him that I just wanted to get a price and that I didn't need any of the other features he was offering, such as the carpet shampooer and floor waxing attachment. He was almost offended that I didn't want to have a complete demonstration and have a portion of my carpet shampooed. I asked him to bring the vacuum without any attachments because I was interested in purchasing just the vacuum. After a fifteen minute haggle session about whether or not I would be willing to sit through a forty-five minute demonstration, he finally and reluctantly agreed to bring the vacuum to my office at a price of $750.

He brought the vacuum into my office and proceeded to unbundle this precious package of his and show me the carpet shampooer, floor polisher and many other attachments. I finally said to him, "I would just like to purchase the vacuum. I have other appointments and would like to complete this transaction." I asked him what the total cost would be and reached for my checkbook. He was grumbling and shaking his head the whole time. As he was leaving, he asked if he could have an appointment with my wife to explain the features of the Kirby G4 vacuum. I made the purchase in spite of his sales efforts. I know that this is an extreme illustration, but sometimes truth is stranger than fantasy.

Uncover a need Recently, I have been involved in interviewing for employees, which is always a stressful situation for the interviewee as well as the interviewer. I like to ask the applicant a question that tells me a lot about their natural sales attributes. What I ask them is: "If you were to make a sale to me, let's say for example sell me a telephone system (and I would point to my phone), how would you go about it?" Then I just wait for a response. Nine times out of ten, the applicant will say, "Well, I would tell you about our telephone system and some of it's features, like how it automatically dials or that it has a speakerphone. I'd also let you know the price of the system and try to answer any questions you might have." Very few applicants are intuitive enough to say to me, "If you are in the market for a telephone system, tell me what your needs are. What is your typical usage of the phone system? What problems are you currently having?" With this approach, you are probing to uncover the need before showing the benefits of the item to the purchaser. The ability to uncover a need is one of the most important parts of the sales process. I would say that 90% of the sales people begin by showing a customer the product or contract and half the time the features that they're showing you don't pertain at all to your needs.

Have a willing client I think we've all had an experience or two at a car dealership, both positive and negative. The classic example is when, upon walking into the car dealership, the salesperson says, "What would it take for me to make a deal with you today on a new car?" Or "If I could find the car you like, at the price you like, could we make a deal today?" Those words make me cringe to think about them. This is the feeling that a lot of our customers have, whether it be insurance, real estate, whatever. They feel like, when they come into your office, they have to be on their guard or something negative could happen to them. This is not the feeling that I want my customers to have. To me, it is so much easier to have a willing participant, a customer that will help you help them.

STOP Selling

START Marketing

Chapter 2

Find your style

Old style sales training, goal setting, rule of numbers and 'just ask' is not an efficient and predictable use of time. I can remember my sales manager asking me to come into his office. He wanted to know my goals for the following month, I had been an insurance agent for two weeks! How was I supposed to know what my goals were? He then proceeded to let me know in no uncertain terms that I wasn't going to make it as an agent unless I got things moving in a much more positive direction.

Well, the old style management tactic of intimidation worked in spite of itself, I never knew that I could work so hard. By the third week, I had exceeded my company imposed quotas. What a relief! But then, guess what? That's right, the phone rang. My manager wanted me to share my sales secrets with my fellow agents in our division. Not only did I not know how I did it, I didn't even have a clue as to how much commission I had earned on these sales. Can you imagine the terror I felt when I had to get up in front of twenty veteran agents and tell them of my new found sales techniques? Or should I say lack thereof.

It had become apparent that flying by the seat of my pants wasn't going to work. I needed a system, an organized approach that could be repeated over and over, month after month. I then set out to find someone who had already developed a sales system that would work for me as well. I talked to all kinds of people and the most common sales system I found was the 'just ask' approach. Just ask a lot of prospects and the sales will come. It's the rule of numbers. This old style sales approach was not efficient enough for me. I knew there had to be a better way. I wanted an organized system, one that would allow me to stay on track and also allow me to expand and perpetuate the system over and over again with predictable results.

As I started trying to develop an effective, organized sales system my mind would tend to wander and my thoughts would go all over the place. I can remember often thinking back to when I was a kid. I remembered fishing with my dad and all the little memories we had shared. Little details like eating moon pies, and Vienna sausage for three days on a camp out. Dad wasn't real organized, but boy was it fun cat fishing and staying up late every night. No one to bother us, no room to clean, just two guys out camping in a tent.

The memories I cherished most were the little simple things that never changed. I would walk out to the end of the dock where the bait shop was and buy one single minnow for my hook. I'd run back to my dad and he would help me place the hook just right into the little fish, the exact same way each and every time. It was predictable, it was solid. I knew I could count on my dad as well as the old man in the bait shack to give me a good lively minnow each time I would show up with a nickel. Looking back now, part of the security of being a kid is knowing that you can rely on things.

These feelings and memories are what became the backbone in my development of a system to bring customers into my insurance agency. It had occurred to me during one of my little wandering daydreams back to when I was a kid, that the predictability of knowing that I could count on the old man at the bait shack was important. He would reach into that cold tank with those rough, thick hands and say to me, "Let's get ya a good lively minna, son" and then I would run back to my dad and he would help me put the hook in just right. This is what I had been searching for; this was the secret of long term customer relationships, *this was the secret of marketing*. I needed a system that would provide a programmed approach to marketing, a system that you can count on day in and day out, a system that creates predictable conditions and predictable results.

Some of the best memories that have come back to me are so small and inconsequential, but in some way have had a lasting impact on my life. I can remember some of our camping escapades where our family would go camping with another family. Their dad worked with my dad. They were a very charismatic group, with three brothers that were all from the South who had quite interesting senses of humor.

I remember one time when our families were camping along the Colorado River. Our dads worked together to build a speedboat. It was made from various used parts that they had come across. They proceeded to launch the boat at the river. Shortly after starting the engine it caught on fire. All of the brothers and my father jumped out of the boat while it was still moving and swam to shore. All we could do was watch the boat burn completely to the waterline and sink, never to be seen again. The maiden voyage lasted all of five minutes, but the brothers and my dad didn't get upset. They laughed about the incident for hours, and were the hit of the campground.

Stories like this have found a soft spot in my heart, and it seems like some of the lessons learned from these escapades are as simple as taking time to find humor and pleasure in everyday business life. The kind of work that I do, where people's lives are literally in my hands, whether it be life insurance, disability insurance, or casualty risk, is a serious and very necessary element of their financial lives. Therefore whenever we can find humor during the day, we must seize the moment.

Seems like, in adversity, oddly enough, humor comes into play. In thinking about humor and life in general, some of my business associates are also personal friends. In fact, there is a group of eight local businessmen who fish together, and as you may have guessed, I am one of them. Once a year, we go fishing at a different location and spend a week laughing and letting our hair down. This therapy seems to draw us closer together every year. The personal experiences that we shared are what bring us together and a point from which to build relationships. All of us should draw on our past experiences and allow them to be useful in our interaction with other people. Use your past experiences! It's all about relationships.

Some of my best sales opportunities were encountered before I became a salesman, such as when I was in high school. I would fix old cars and sell them. My mother would come out into the garage and there would be paint all over the garage floor and on her washing machine. The poor woman would just stand there with a disgusted look on her face. I would tell her, "Mom, it's okay. I have this one sold". Before I was twenty years old, I had bought and sold thirty-two vehicles. I then went on to college and worked summers for the U.S. Forest Service. During that time I kept feeling unfulfilled. One day it occurred to me that I enjoyed working with people and selling, as I remembered my teen-age years with the cars. Needless to say, I was a salesman and didn't realize it. All of these personal experiences help to develop your "salespersonality".

STOP

Selling

START

Marketing

Chapter 3

Building Client Relationships

In business, building relationships is the number one priority, because once a solid relationship is in place, price is no longer a priority in your client's mind. The added value of the client relationship transcends cost. To me, there's no higher compliment than to have your client say to you that they put their complete trust and confidence in you to help them make the proper decision about a purchase. Trust and confidence is the key to building a long-term client relationship. Only through honest, fair dealings can this be accomplished. In doing this, your reputation will be self-evident after a while. It is hard to please everyone all the time, but someone who is doing an honest job and being fair to everyone concerned can't help but develop a good reputation.

Get involved There are ways to enhance your company's reputation through outward exposure in the community, such as volunteering for the Chamber of Commerce, or helping non-profit organizations, or becoming involved in the community in some other way. This involvement should be done in ways that you feel qualified. In other words, if you are a financial planner, help the budget committee for the hospital, or help them understand gifting principles, charitable remainder trusts and that kind of thing. If you are a CPA, help them with spreadsheets and budgeting. Become known as a professional in your field by allowing others to see you in that role.

Look the part I see people all the time in professional business that don't look like professionals. To me, half of the battle is exhibiting professionalism through your dress, your office, even your car. Everything that you are involved in should reinforce the fact that you are a professional.

If I hire an attorney, I expect him to be in a suit, and to be in a professional looking office. Or, if I'm having someone build a home, I want him to be a professional licensed contractor. I feel like a lot of business people are having to work extra hard just to overcome some of the negative connotations that they project to their clients through their dress, mannerisms, and the condition of their business environment.

Plant some seeds In the sales process, not all sales are made on the first contact. In some cases, the salesperson needs to plant a seed in the prospect's mind for a future sale. This can be done in many ways.

It can be done even as a casual verbal comment as a local real estate broker made to me one time. I had just recently purchased a rental unit from this man and after we signed the offer, I was walking out of the office, saying goodbye to him and his staff. He walked to the door with me, and just before I left, he said, "Tom, thank you for allowing me to help you with this transaction. I know it will be the first of many future transactions."

As I got in the car, I didn't really think about it much, but about a month later, when the escrow closed, he asked me to come in to the office for a few minutes. When I arrived, he had three other rental properties laid out on the desk with photos and descriptions.

He told me that he received the listing and thought of me because of the close proximity to the first property that I had purchased. He thought it would be convenient for me to check on them all at one time and to have a consolidated group of units. Although the deal looked good, I was not in the position to purchase additional units at that time. He told me that he would continue to look and that in the future we would get together to reevaluate my real estate investment portfolio.

To this day, he and I have developed a business relationship that revolves around respect and commitment due to the added value of his professionalism and thoughtfulness, as well as planting the seed in my mind that we would do future transactions. It was almost a subliminal inference that I would do business with him in the future.

Keep in touch Another way to plant seeds is to continue contact through letters to your client base. We pend a three contact schedule in our computer so that at least three times a year, the client is either called or sent some kind of material that continues to hold our product and brandname in front of the client. The scheduled contacts provide me with the opportunity to inform a client of additional benefits that we may have available and in so doing, continues to keep our name in their thought processes at all times during the year.

Brand names Only recently, brand recognition has become a big buzzword in most industries. For years and years, it was being utilized, although I don't think it was totally planned as it is today. We all remember the Union 76 ball, the big yellow Shell and, of course, the flying Mobil horse. I'm sure you remember what type of fuel that you used in your car by the brand or icon at the service station. Of course, nowadays with the price of fuel, and the fact that most of us don't have time to go to the same service station all the time, we pretty much look at fuel as a generic product.

Although the brands are still available, they seem to have blurred over recent years. I feel that brand recognition can help only if it conjures up feelings of loyalty or added value. A brand name equating to quality products or services is becoming less of a fact as industries continue to cut services and quality in their competition for market share. As with the automobile service station, since they don't wash your windows or check your oil, you might as well go generic.

I don't want to paint a picture that says brand name products aren't worth the cost, but just the opposite. I like brand name goods. They are usually of better quality and the company will stand behind their product to protect their good name. For this reason, planting seeds about the quality of your product during the sale will help foster feelings of quality, integrity and added value for years to come.

STOP Selling

START Marketing

Chapter 4

Know how to communicate with your client

Over the years, I have picked up many different phrases or ways to spur interest from a client. For example, when I'm meeting with a certain group, such as marketing Tax Sheltered Annuities with schoolteachers, a key phrase would be, "What most of your associates are doing is a diversified portfolio in a tax sheltered annuity. Would this be of interest to you as well?" Another phrase for this same kind of situation would be, "Normally what we recommend for clients similar to yourselves is...," or "As a general rule most of your fellow educators have taken advantage of the tax sheltered annuity as a way to supplement their retirement." Draw on phrases to keep things on track.

Listen to your client Most sales people fail to listen to what the client is telling them. We all ask our questions to get a response from the client, but fail to hear their answers. We're too busy thinking of the next question to ask. All questions can be asked in two different ways, one more effective than the other. The first way requires a direct response from the client, usually a yes or no. The second would be an open ended type of question that requires a more complete response from the client. The indirect type question is thought provoking and should evoke more of a detailed answer than the direct type question. The answer will be more of an emotional response rather than a technical or calculated yes or no answer.

Avoid the dead end Many young sales people ask direct questions, and when the answer comes back as a yes or no, they are put into a stressful mode where they have to immediately come up with another question. It begins to look like an interrogation rather than a sale beginning to happen. It is always uncomfortable when you are doing all the asking, and the client is just sitting there with his arms folded.

Getting your clients to help you help them is the key to successful selling. They need to know that you are acting on their behalf or trying to help them with the decision making process. Selling should be enjoyable, not a stressful or adversarial process. You need to develop ways to foster this feeling among your clients so that you make more sales, and so your job becomes easier and more enjoyable.

Recently, I had two totally different appointments. One appointment was very tense and unproductive, the second was a lot of fun and the clients actually told me that they enjoyed coming in and meeting with me. There were two totally different feelings produced by the clients and myself.

I guess the difference would have to be in the personalities of the clients, because I feel my demeanor was the same with both. In thinking it through, about the only thing I could come up with would be to take a pass on the first client and to focus on the second one.

Eliminate those clients who are unwilling to be helpful, your time is valuable and these clients are the least likely to respond positively to your efforts. Focus on those who want you to help them.

Remember give them a chance before you walk away, some clients need more time than others to warm up to you. Your staff will also be able to help pre-qualify the appointments, this should be discussed as part of your marketing stratigies. Pre-qualifing clients will make your job much smoother and allow more time for actual sales.

STOP Selling

START Marketing

Chapter 5

Marketing Plan

Developing an organized approach to marketing your product or service is the key to consistent sales. Regardless of the service or product, a written automatic system must exist in order to make those consistent sales. I can remember calling on clients many times without an organized system. Alphabetically, starting with the letter 'A', we would call those people on our list . Then we would get busy with something else, and leave it for a month or two. When we came back to the call list, we would have forgotten where we left off, and begin with 'A' again. I'm sure the Abbott family got sick of our calls!

A programmed approach starts with developing a full database on your current clientele as well as prospective clients. This database will allow you to select criteria within target groups to focus your contacts and automatically provides you with contact lists, creating an ongoing process. It really is an excellent way to stay organized.

Your database should contain basic information about the client such as full name, address, phone numbers, as well as past purchases from your company.

A printed "call list" should be used for taking notes while talking with the prospect and procuring the appointment. Provide ample room on the page for your notes, including a place to note the date and time of calls made to individual clients.

Three steps to success It is my feeling that some kind of pre-approach is necessary prior to actually presenting the product or service to the customer. In order to pre qualify the prospect, a three step process is needed: (1) a pre-approach letter, (2) follow-up call and then (3) securing an appointment. Once this has been done and the client comes in to meet with you the majority of the work is done. The prospect is now willing to work with you and help you help them in making their purchase.

First the pre-approach letter should be sent to the clients. The contact lists your database provides will organize the process and make it very easy to maintain. You will need the pre-approach letters to go out on a regular and continuous schedule. Make your follow-up calls one week after the letters have gone out. Be sure you do not wait any longer than one week to make this call, or your warm call will turn cold again.

To secure an appointment I feel that it is important for someone other than the salesperson to initiate and set up the appointment. If the salesperson initiates the call and sets up the appointment, the prospect generally will ask questions and expect you to do a mini sale on the phone, which will never work. Or they'll say that you should send them more information in the mail so they can review it and get back to you. The goal is to set up an appointment that will allow you a face-to-face meeting with the prospect. Only then can you properly council them as to how your product or service fits their needs.

A well organized and up-to-date database is the key, you need to be working on it regularly. Schedule a certain number of letters and calls each week, this should become a weekly, ongoing process. Keep notes on each of the calls to your clients, staying current and timely as well as adding new prospects to your list on a regular basis. Maintaining your list and using it are the most important ways to achieve those regular and consistent sales that make for success.

Follow-up Looking back over the years, from a customer's perspective, I have never had a call from a car dealership, or furniture store or any other type of business and been asked if I would like to consider purchasing a new item. It seems to me that any business should encourage it's sales staff to keep a client file and touch base with the clients once a year, either with a letter or phone call or maybe a brochure on the new product line. This would be a way to insulate their current clients from moving to another competitor or store as well as plant those seeds which may lead to future sales or upgrades. I know it would impress me if a company called, or sent me a letter once a year saying, "Hey, when you are ready for your next purchase, please think of us."

Our last office remodel is a good example of a lost opportunity. It was about ten years ago and it was pretty obvious that we were in line for a furniture upgrade or at least a review of our furnishings, and possibly changing a few items to freshen up the look. Wouldn't it have been nice if an interior design company had called us or sent us a letter saying that they wanted to remind us that they were available if we wanted to change our look, or replace or upgrade any worn furnishings? Instead, we called them. Two days later they called back and put us off for another two weeks. In the meantime, we decided to just go out and look at some office furniture. We ended up doing the redo ourselves. Again, if the design company had a programmed approach utilizing a client database, a prompt follow-up could more easily be made to prevent those kinds of missed opportunities.

We use a computer generated master file for each client that indicates contacts that have been made to them over the years, with a date of the contact and a notation as to what was discussed, or which letter was sent out to them. To me, an organized marketing plan includes developing this kind of database . It will provide an automatic positive contact system for you. Look back at your own experiences as a customer. Wouldn't it have been nice to have been contacted or at least have had some interest shown to you as a client from one year to the next? I feel that it is imperative that this kind of system be a part of any overall marketing plan.

Keeping your clients People want to feel that they are cared for, they want you to call on them. Don't think that you are bothering them. This can be just a friendly call. I can remember my sister-in-law saying how impressed she was when her banker called her personally to review her accounts and tell her about some new services offered by the bank.

More sales ideas Another thing we do is to keep a list of sales ideas. I add to it whenever I hear of one that I think is a good one. Here are a few:

1. If you are worrying about 10% of your clients that are difficult 90% of the time, and only 10% of your time is spent worrying over the other 90%, consider removing that difficult 10%.
2. Don't be afraid to follow your hunches.
3. Don't tell people what they need.
4. Always think of the client's best interests, not which one makes you the most money.
5. Maintain a sales information binder with proof sources and examples of your product or service. I carry one with me whenever I'm meeting with a client.
6. Keep in mind how you want to be perceived. If you're not living up to that perception, then be prepared to change.
7. Work on skills to help you figure out what people really want and need.
8. Find ways to become closer to the clients that you should be spending time with. Work with your preferred target groups.
9. Decide what your market is and target that market.
10. Make appointments in a professional manner so you feel like a counselor and not a salesman.
11. Use perpetual marketing systems.

Selling and marketing is not an exact science. There are so many ways to accomplish your goals. Setting yourself apart from the others is important and sometimes it is the little things you do that make the big difference.

Target your market Developing new clients is best accomplished though a targeted marketing approach. In other words, find a group that best fits the service or product that you are offering. Or better yet, search through a computer database for people who would most likely be interested in that product or service you offer. This search can be based on different criteria such as home ownership, income, employment, etc.

Once an initial contact is made, if there is no interest move on to the next prospect. Don't waste time on a disinterested prospect. If there is some interest then the next step should be securing that first appointment. Once the appointment is made, then interest can be assumed and the majority of the sale has been made.

Fill the need It's my opinion that selling is nothing more than fulfilling a need; to help the client get what he or she wants. The biggest and most important part of the sales process is having the prospect say that they want to actually meet with you. That's what I feel should be the main objective in the marketing plan, not product knowledge or features or benefits of the product or service. That comes after they have agreed to meet with you. In having the prospective client meet with you, especially at your office, the prospect is committed and 90% of the sale is made. You now have a customer who is a willing participant.

The next step is getting the prospect involved in the decision making and allowing them to feel comfortable working with you to fulfill the need. In other words, the salesperson is basically a facilitator to help the prospect fill the need that they have. A willing participant in the sale is a customer who wants to talk with you about a need they have. They need to feel that you can provide them with information that will help them make an informed decision.

Willing and comfortable To be a willing participant, the prospect has to feel comfortable and know that the salesperson has their best interests in mind. Many things can lead up to a prospect having trust and confidence in the salesperson. First among these are professional office or store surroundings with a knowledgeable and caring staff. Repeatable and predictable results require the sales staff to be constantly improving on their professionalism, constantly showing the sincerity and the willingness to help clients with their needs.

I have found that even the small things can contribute to a successful, professional operation. For example, the way the staff dresses, the appearance of the office or store, the physical layout; a clean and comfortable atmosphere is of great importance. We have found that an outside consultant firm that looks at color scheme, furniture, office layout and customer flow is a big benefit. Sometimes it is good to have an outside person look at your operation to make sure that you're not missing the forest because of the trees so to speak. This kind of extra effort will pay off because you only have one chance to make that important first impression and sometimes the smallest details can make or break a sale.

If an outside consulting firm is not available, have a friend that works with the public in a similar business give an opinion on your business environment. Another great way to get office layout ideas is to visit other firms and just look for the good and bad features.

STOP
Selling
START
Marketing

STOP Selling

START Marketing

Chapter 6

Alternative Marketing

Seminar sales are becoming more popular with service type products such as insurance, real estate, and financial services. Seminar selling allows the salesperson to present the product to many people at one time. The key to successful seminar selling is understanding that people feel more comfortable in an educational setting, rather than in a one-on-one sales appointment.

The seminar should take on several characteristics - but most importantly it should be educational. You must provide information on topics that provide the range and breadth of topics that will attract a broad group of prospects. Equally important is the seminar's need to be relevant to the various groups and address the needs and lifestyles of those in attendance.

It is not easy setting up a seminar. The prospects must come from a database or segment of the population that would be most likely to have an interest in the subject that you want to present. An invitation should be sent out with a personal signature, inviting the prospects to come to the educational presentation. Some type of refreshment should be included.

I found that heavy hors d'oeuvres, wine and soft drinks work best because the guests can mingle and discuss things with the other people at the presentation as well as sit at their seats and enjoy the refreshments while you're speaking. I've found that a complete dinner is very cumbersome and ends up taking way too long. Invariably, someone doesn't get served in time and hard feelings can ensue.

Two speakers seem to work best. It gives the audience a variety, as well as giving a dual billing on the agenda. This also allows you to network with other professionals that have similar but slightly different products or services. In other words, a retirement seminar that includes a CPA as well as a mutual fund representative would allow both disciplines to invite participants to attend. It gives you twice the client base as well as two diversified presentations that together will provide participants a fuller understanding of your products or services. Your clients meet the other speaker, and you meet some of his or her clients. It is a great way to enhance both of your practices by bringing in new business.

I have spoken at seminars and motivational workshops over the years and really enjoy most audiences they are a joy to work with; others are more subdued or not very interactive. I can remember one sales seminar in particular where I spoke. From the very moment I arrived at the site, I was greeted and made comfortable. I felt appreciated. The audience was great and interacted with me very well. They were interested, and I feel they got a lot out of the session. It was a joy for me to work with them. Some audiences are not as receptive.

At first, I was inclined to just write it off as nice people versus not so nice people. But I also felt that perhaps some time could be spent looking more closely and trying to analyze the differences so that I could draw on those concepts in the future, and possibly encourage or enhance a more positive feeling in a group or individual setting when things are not going well.

Trying to determine what makes audiences so different is very difficult, I believe a key to the overall mood is the desire and willingness on the part of the audience to become involved in the presentation.

The jury is still out on this subject, any in-depth review of "audience personality" is hard to relate to. However, these days of mass marketing require that we delve into the psychology of our markets.

Learn when to let them go Not only can we market to specific demographics with our client base, we might also consider including in our client criteria the notion of the pleasant prospect. Maybe there is a way that we could include some kind of notation on the attitude of the client. I must say that in writing this book, I have come up with some subtle and sometimes obscure thoughts about marketing.

Brainstorming ideas I think that the idea of brainstorming and not ruling out any options can be very helpful in developing your marketing plan. Your staff should be involved in the brainstorming session. This will allow for team building and for the staff to buy in on the plan. Remember the sky is the limit in a good brainstorming session.

Go to the web The internet can be a tool in marketing. It allows you to reach a large group of prospective clients. However, it is somewhat cold and impersonal. Let's not let the internet take over our position in the marketplace. Let's use it to help bring in a new type of purchaser. When it comes to insurance, real estate, securities, etc. people already have a somewhat negative or apprehensive and cautionary view of the whole idea of purchasing any of these items. Couple that with the apprehension of the unknown involved in the internet and cyberspace and it can make for a very uneasy transaction.

It is necessary that, as a marketing person, we show the added value of the personal relationship. There is a lot of hype nowadays about the internet and how it will take over many of our jobs. I've watched for this and have found in my own experience and that of others, the Internet simply cannot replace the human relationships that are so important to the sales industry.

The internet has it's place, it has a vast amount of information and immediate access to problem solving applications, information for medical science, and technology.

However, when it comes to a one on one relationship with a sales representative, the internet is nothing more than a cold clammy handshake that gives no warm feelings to a purchaser.

The internet has its flaws, my oldest daughter Jenny recently bought a dog leash that somehow attaches to the back of her mountain bike so that she can exercise her Doberman without having her arm pulled out of the socket while riding her bicycle. She is 18 years old and feels very comfortable on the computer and the internet. Our first internet purchase was this dog leash which was ordered two months ago and billed to my Visa card. The leash still has not come in, although the item has been processed and billed on the card. So we have paid our money, and have not received the product.

It is very rewarding at least in some way for me to tell my daughter "I told you so, the internet is not what it is cracked up to be". Well, being the teenager that she is, naturally she defended the internet and said that there must have been some problem with the shipping or UPS delivery. I feel that time will tell and that if we do our jobs with sincerity and conviction, and continue to show the added value and benefits of dealing with a real person, the sales force in America will prevail over the electronic order taker called the internet.

The good and the bad Although the internet has it's limitations with regard to the personal touch, it does allow businesses to spread their brand name over a large international platform. Another benefit of the internet is that it does give you a record of the so called 'hits' on your web site which allows you as a business to evaluate a certain target of the market. This gives you a built in database or at least a customer profile. The internet is on one hand an unbelievably exciting marketing tool, and on the other hand, can be very frustrating and impersonal.

Another way to get the word out Most of us think of advertisement as a way to get the word out about a product or service that we offer. That may be the case with some products or services, but in studying the benefits of advertising I've found that the actual advertisement itself does not bring customers in. What advertisement will do is give name or brand recognition so that when the person needs a product or service that you have, they will think of your company. If the brand is etched into their mind deep enough, they will come to you.

Don't be in a hurry to see results. In our local newspaper, we have an advertisement opportunity called TOMA, Top of the Mind Awareness. The philosophy is for you to have a small ad in the newspaper at least twice per week, so that people continue to see your brand or name. It is not meant to advertise a particular product or service, but rather your company's identity . This is so that, month after month, and year after year, the people see the company name and it gives them awareness. When they need the product or service, hopefully they will remember your name or company.

Advertisement can be so subjective and in most cases results cannot be tracked very well. It took three weeks before my wife noticed my TOMA ad in our local paper, even with a photo of me! So don't expect immediate results.

Television ads are effective in some cases, as will as radio broadcasts, but as I have mentioned before, it takes time to imprint the brand, or name of the company. A consistent long-term planned approach works best in advertising, not just a quick short-term blitz.

An advertising plan is essential, it is almost like it hurts you if you don't advertise even if you don't see it helping you right away. Most successful companies have some sort of advertisement plan.

An example of the effectiveness of advertisement and brand recognition can be found in my youngest daughter Julie's closet. The majority of her clothes are branded and believe me all of her friends notice if she wears what they refer to as "generic" or non-brandname clothes. I'm sure alot of thought goes into branding for teens.

STOP
Selling

START
Marketing

Chapter 7

Slump breakers and shakers

At certain times, it seems like a salesperson gets into a slump where it just isn't fun anymore. I think we've all had times like that. I've tried to develop a way to identify this and then to take action to mitigate it's impact. When I see that I'm becoming negative, or seeing the glass half empty, I try to stop the bleeding, so to speak, by getting back to the basics of what I enjoy most and that is meeting one on one with the customers. The day to day paperwork and employee concerns as well as an unhappy customer, billing problems and the like can really get a person down. What I find that works best to break a slump is to get together with the staff and develop a short-term incentive to meet a goal for production and to make it fun. Sometimes we just need to refocus our energy in a positive way.

One interesting note: the term 'slump breaker' was coined by a man that worked with me, in fact he was a company executive, whom I very much respected. He is retired now, but I know if he reads this book, he will get a chuckle. I think we can all relate at one time or another to the misery of a slump.

I can relate this to golfing as well. As an avid golfer, I know the feeling of trying so hard, but no matter what you do, the 'golf gods' don't always look down favorably upon you. The harder you try, the worse it gets. Sometimes it's better to get back to basics and remember that you're only here once, and you should try to enjoy every minute to the fullest. Just like golf, your work should be enjoyable. If it isn't, you should change your work. In the sales field, you don't have to move to another company to do this. Just move to a new client. Each client becomes a unique opportunity to refresh your career and to allow you to reap rewards in the future.

Keep the mental edge Over the years, I find myself in and out of optimum productivity. One day, my sales are setting the world on fire and the next day, I'm just not in the mood. Sometimes you can't explain why, but the sales will just not happen. Other times, things seem so easy. I sat down to try to figure this out and to try to turn this into a positive learning experience. In brainstorming this, I found that when a salesperson's mind starts to wander to other outside distractions and becomes out of focus with the task at hand, it only takes a simple mental reminder to get back in the groove again.

It has always been my philosophy that there is a time and place for everything. For example, my mom always told me that when you are in church, you pray. When you are watching a ball game, you watch the game. When you work, you work. You can't do one thing if your thinking about the other.

Organize your time Staying focused is always difficult for a salesperson because most good salespeople are free spirits with emotional needs that can be easily misdirected. It is important to set aside time for productive sales activities and to also set aside time for diversions. In my own insurance business, I've found that working two day intervals with at least half a day away during the middle of the week works best for me. Not that I don't put in my forty hours a week, I'm sure the average is way more than that! A salesperson works in spurts or is productive in spurt time, unlike a service oriented worker who might be more organized and can pace themselves.

The salesperson is more like a racehorse or sprinter and knowing that, you must devise ways to keep the sales force focused and concentrating on the task at hand. One way to do this is to have certain times set aside that encourage and facilitate good sales activities. One way to kick off a sales campaign is to have a call night where all of the sales team gathers together in one room with several phones and call from a pre-arranged prospect list. The camaraderie and peer pressure enhances the effort. Bring in pizza and soft drinks to keep the atmosphere fun, we have even gone over the edge by dressing up in different costumes. For an example, we had a western night where everyone dressed like cowboys. You should have seen some of the city boys in their western attire! We had more fun that night, and in fact, we had our management people from the home office come out and join in the fun. It was a very productive evening and kicked off our sales campaign in a big way.

Any excuse that will cause your team, or yourself to focus on the marketing task is helpful. Try to determine what best fits your team and try to continue to use these incentives to further build your sales.

Rejuvenate yourself Have you ever wondered why in the fire department, the firemen work two days on and two days off, two days on, then four days off? The reason for this is that it gives them an opportunity to regroup and rejuvenate themselves physically and emotionally so that they can handle the rigors of fire fighting and emergency responses. This same kind of rejuvenation is necessary for a salesperson to achieve their best results.

Like the racehorse, salespeople must be ready to go at all times and when the gun fires they have to be going at one hundred percent. Even when you go to your local store after work, you have to be 'on'. You never know when one of your customers is going to come up to you and say "Hi". Your time is not really your own. You never know when you may be asked for information about your product, or when an opportunity may appear for a sales appointment.

A good way to refresh and rejuvenate yourself is to have small diversionary episodes in your day and through the week. For an example, check to see what your best hours of the day are. When are you on and when are you at your best? Keep a log, or have a staff person observe your most productive and least productive times of the day. Then structure your schedule around these most productive times. For an example, if you are a morning person, why not have your appointments in the morning so that you're in your best frame of mind during the time that you're with your clients.

Take a break Once a week I take a couple of hours away from the office to just unwind with friends or family. When you are self-employed, you probably work more hours over all than a salaried employee and you need to be able to get away. We should be in control of our time and lives. Don't let your sales career become a super full time job.

Salespeople that are employed by a company do not always have the flexibility to get away from the office or away from their sales activities for a rejuvenation break, but there are ways to divert your mind and relieve stress even if you can't get away from the place of business.

We are all allowed some time to read and study, therefore I feel that when you need to refresh, a good way is to read motivational material related to your profession. Sometimes just a fifteen minute read will help you get the juices going again. A small short diversion can last many times it's length in productivity.

Be flexible I also feel that a salesperson cannot get by with a two-week vacation once a year. Remember, salespeople generally are not endurance runners; they are sprinters and need to store up energy so that when the gun goes off they can hit the ground running. Perhaps spreading vacation time out a little more over the course of the year would be more helpful, such as ten three-day weekends rather than one two-week vacation.

Encourage your supervisor or the person you report to, to treat you like a racehorse. Give them the hints that they need. Make them think it is their idea to give you flexible schedules or to spread your vacation time out more so you come back to work refreshed and ready to go. This is the way to increase your productivity.

As I drive to my office today after being on a three day trip, I feel refreshed and ready to go with a positive attitude and in a result oriented direction. After this short vacation and this feeling of rejuvenation, I almost feel I should call ahead to the office to warn them that I'm on my way! My point is, take care of yourself. Plan for recreation and diversion mentally and physically.

The sales opportunity is a great life, and an honorable profession, but you have to take care of yourself and plan ways to rejuvenate and release the stress associated with working with the public each and every day. Nobody said it would be easy but as someone once said, "If it is too easy, it is probably not worth going after". We should all look forward and prepare ourselves so that we can meet and embrace our challenges.

STOP
Selling
START
Marketing

STOP
Selling

START
Marketing

Chapter 8

Give a hand, get a hand

In sales and marketing, sometimes the energy level is just not there. Sometimes we just don't feel like we can do what is required of us. It is times like this that I try to contact someone else in my field that maybe has less experience than me, such as a new salesperson that I have met. I like to call to encourage them and hope that some of their energy will rub off on me. Rather than sit around and make excuses for myself, a little click goes off in my mind, and I immediately go to some sort of diversion. If there are others in your field that would look up to you for advice, then give them a call. When a new salesperson starts, give them a call or stop by and see them that day. Give someone encouragement and you will receive some of their energy for your trouble. Sometimes all it takes is a little positive feedback for us to get the juices flowing again.

Just say thanks Another trick that I have learned to combat fatigue is to call on your good customers to just say "thank you". Don't sell them anything, don't even mention a new product line, just call to check in with them. In the insurance business, when I start to feel overwhelmed, I simply call someone that has been helped by our insurance company on a claim and listen to the positive comments to absorb some of that positive energy.

The better you are, the easier it gets Have you ever noticed that when things are really clicking, it is almost like you're just letting it happen? It is effortless. No matter what you do, good things happen. Well, I know this doesn't last long so embrace those times and try to recall them, recall that good feeling you had as much as possible. One thing I've noticed over the years is that the better a salesperson is, the easier it looks. Sometimes athletes are so good, a fantastic play, catch or shot doesn't really look that fantastic on TV because it appears so effortless. When I watch the golf channel and see how smooth the professional golfers swing, it almost looks like they're swinging at half speed. Bottom line, the easier it looks the better the golfer or salesperson undoubtedly is.

In marketing, you are looking at a broad base of prospects and trying to figure out ways to allow the prospects to do business with you. In selling, you are actually exchanging the product for a price. Both can be viewed similarly to sports. If it looks like an effort to the people watching it, it probably will not be received as well. If it looks and feels effortless to the prospects, it undoubtedly will be received in a better light.

Sometimes we try too hard and in doing so, maybe we don't listen or pick up on the subtle nuances that the customers are giving us. I believe one of the most common mistakes that I see in a young salesperson is that they don't listen to what the prospect wants to tell them. They are so busy thinking of what they're going to say next, that they really never hear what the prospect is trying to say. It makes the sale look cumbersome, which in turn gives the prospect an uneasy feeling and makes the sale that much harder.

It happens to all of us when we start to feel ourselves dominating the conversation. A little click needs to go off in our minds that says, "Hey, wait a minute, lets get back on track". Maybe a little key phrase could be used when this happens, such as, "Excuse me, tell me what you think about this." Just something to give you a clue to catch yourself before you get in too deep and possibly lose the sale.

STOP Selling

START Marketing

Chapter 9

In summary, some closing thoughts

The words that I have written in this book have simply been a compilation of things that I've learned and gleaned from others over the years. Life's experiences determine how each person relates to other people in their jobs or business or just in every day life. I hope this book has helped identify some of the experiences in your own life that can help you go forward in your career. We all have a vision of what we want our life to be like. I hope that your vision will be realized and that you will be able to help others in their lives. In doing so, you will in some way help the world to be a better place.

Life goes so fast and it seems the older you get, the faster the years go by. Our world is changing so rapidly through technology that I can't even imagine what things will develop in the next ten or twenty years. One thing is sure, people will always need to purchase products and services. Therefore, we can be sure marketing and sales will continue to be a viable profession.

Let's all try to make it a noble profession and continue to upgrade our standing in society through professional conduct with each and every customer.

STOP
Selling

START
Marketing